Get Wise

Bullying

⊖ why does it happen?

Sarah Medina

Heinemann
LIBRARY

www.heinemann.co.uk/library
Visit our website to find out more information about **Heinemann Library** books.

To order:
☎ Phone 44 (0) 1865 888066
🖹 Send a fax to 44 (0) 1865 314091
🖥 Visit the Heinemann Bookshop at www.heinemann.co.uk/library to browse our catalogue and order online.

First published in Great Britain by Heinemann Library,
Halley Court, Jordan Hill, Oxford OX2 8EJ, part of Harcourt
Education.

Heinemann is a registered trademark of Harcourt
Education Ltd.

© Harcourt Education Ltd 2004
First published in paperback in 2005

The moral right of the proprietor has been asserted.

Editorial: Lucy Thunder and Helen Cannons
Design: David Poole and Kamae Design
Illustrations: Jeff Anderson
Picture Research: Rebecca Sodergren and
Kay Altwegg
Production: Edward Moore

Originated by Repro Multi-Warna
Printed and bound in China by WKT Company Limited

The paper used to print this book comes from sustainable
resources.
ISBN 0 431 21003 9 (hardback)
08 07 06 05 04
10 9 8 7 6 5 4 3 2
ISBN 0 431 21009 8 (paperback)
09 08 07 06 05
10 9 8 7 6 5 4 3 2 1

British Library Cataloguing in Publication Data
Medina, Sarah
Bullying – how does it happen? – (Get wise)
371.5'8
A full catalogue record for this book is available from the
British Library.

Acknowledgements

The Publishers would like to thank the following for
permission to reproduce photographs: John Birdsall pp. **8**,
16; Bubbles pp.**22**, **26**, /Pauline Cutter p.**12**; Corbis p.**6**,
/RF p.**17**, **21**; Sally and Richard Greenhill p.**15**; Kidscape
p.**27**; Alexander McIntyre p.**20**; Photofusion p.**9**, /Clarissa
Leahy pp.**5**, **13**, /Brian Mitchell p.**24**, /Ulrike Preuss p.**7**;
John Walmsley pp.**18**, **19**, **25**; Janine Wiedel p.**10**; Zefa/G.
Boden p.**28**.

Cover photograph of a girl by the roadside, reproduced
with permission of Alexander McIntyre.

Quotes and news items are taken from a variety of
sources, including: BBC news, BBCi Newsround and the
United Nations Pachamama website. Special thanks to
ChildLine for the case study information used on pp.9, 29.

The Publishers would like to thank Andrew Mellor of the
Anti-Bullying Network for his assistance in the preparation
of this book.

Every effort has been made to contact copyright holders
of any material reproduced in this book. Any omissions
will be rectified in subsequent printings if notice is given
to the Publishers.

Disclaimer

Important note: If you are being
bullied and need help, go straight to
the Getting help box on page 31.
There are phone numbers to call for
immediate help and support.

Contents

Words appearing in bold, **like this**, are explained in the Glossary.

Bullying - the lowdown

What is bullying – and how can it be stopped?

Bullying happens a lot. From the UK to Australia, someone will know someone who has been bullied at some time in their life. You may be surprised to learn that it does not just happen to children, either. Adults can be bullied, too. But no one – not a single person – has to live with bullying, and it is definitely possible to stop it.

What is bullying?

Bullying is when somebody goes out of their way to hurt another person. They may do this over and over again, or just once – but it is still bullying. Bullies hurt others in many different ways – from beating them up to taking their friends away. **Physical bullying** includes hitting, kicking, pushing and stealing things. **Non-physical bullying** includes name-calling, gossiping and leaving people out. Bullying can even happen from a distance – **e-bullying**, by email or mobile phone, is becoming more common.

Down – but not out

Bullying hurts. People who are bullied often feel unhappy and lonely. They may be anxious, and worried that there is something wrong with them. Some **victims** of bullying can become very **depressed** – they may run away from home or, rarely, even try to kill themselves. However, with lots of help and support from others, it is possible to bring bullying to an end.

Calling a halt

No one asks to be bullied – and no one deserves to be bullied, either. Fortunately, people can work together to stop bullying. There is lots of advice about stopping bullying in this book. In the UK and Australia, all schools should have an **anti-bullying policy**, which explains how the school will help if a pupil is being bullied. We all have a responsibility to help people who are being bullied, so that they no longer feel alone – or helpless.

🎧 Bullying can make people feel very alone and frightened.

Newsflash

Studies have shown that more than a third of children with mobile phones have received name-calling text messages. One in every ten pupils at UK primary schools says that they have received a hurtful or **threatening** text. Bullies can also set up 'hate' websites, where they spread rumours about their victims. There are fears that this form of bullying will increase.

Top thoughts

'It's everybody's responsibility to prevent bullying.'

Malcolm Irons (Deputy headteacher, UK)

Who are the bullies – and the victims of bullying?

Bullying can happen at home, at school, in the community, and even in the workplace. Boys and men can bully others – and so can girls and women. Anyone can be a **victim** of bullying, too. Bullying is horrible for everyone – but the good news is that bullying can be stopped.

Big bullies, little bullies

Bullies can come in all shapes and sizes. Adults can bully other adults – and children. Children can bully other children – and even adults! Often, people bully in groups, because it makes them feel safer and more powerful. And even though it may only be the group leader who hits out at or laughs at their victim, those who stand by and watch are part-bullying, too. No matter who the bully is, or why he or she bullies, bullying is always wrong.

Newsflash

Children really can bully adults. A new report in the UK says that more parents are getting bullied by their own kids. Shouting, spitting, punching, kicking and **threatening** family members are just some of the things parents are worried about. Mums are bullied most. And there is not much difference between boys or girls – both can be serious bullies. Boys and girls aged thirteen to fifteen are the most violent. But boys aged nine to twelve are also guilty of being bullies to their parents.

All sorts of people use bullying behaviour – and it can happen anywhere and at any time.

Talk time

Who do you think gets bullied at school?

ali: Kids who are new at school sometimes get bullied.

Lauren: Probably because they haven't had a chance to make friends yet – or they may be shy.

Maribel: Anyone who is different can get bullied, really.

Tyrone: Yes – like people who look different, or talk differently – or who are of a different **race**. Or if they have a disability or need extra help at school.

Lauren: You can even get bullied if you're too clever!

ali: Yeah – bullies are sometimes just jealous of people, for whatever reason.

🎧 We can stop bullying by getting along with each other, no matter how different we are.

THINK IT THROUGH

Is someone who watches a person being picked on a bully themselves?

Yes. If you don't speak out against the bullying, it's as if you are joining in with it.

No. Sometimes, it can be hard to stand up to a bully – you might get picked on yourself.

What do YOU think?

How do people bully others?

Fact Flash

If physical bullying leads to bruising, cuts, swelling and a bleeding nose, it is called 'actual bodily harm', and it can be reported to the police.

Boys are more ➲ likely to bully physically, by hitting or kicking their victim. People who watch are part of the bullying, even if they do not do the hitting themselves.

People bully others in all sorts of ways. No matter how they do it, bullies make themselves feel more powerful by making their **victim** feel small. Boys bully other boys, and they bully girls, too. They are more likely to use **physical bullying**, such as hitting or kicking. Girls usually bully other girls, and they often use **non-physical bullying** – for example, gossiping and **e-bullying**. Both physical and non-physical bullying are hurtful – and wrong.

Getting physical

Have you ever seen anyone hit, kick, push, bite or spit at someone else? These are forms of physical bullying. Physical bullying is frightening. Even the **threat** of it can make someone feel very scared. Other kinds of physical bullying include damaging someone's belongings, such as their clothes or books, and stealing from them. Bullies have even been known to lock their victims in or out of a place.

Words, words, words

Non-physical bullying hurts people differently from – but just as much as – physical bullying. This form of bullying includes calling people names, teasing, threatening and ignoring people and embarrassing them in front of others – and generally being mean. Bullies may make up false stories about someone, just to get them into trouble. They may try to make someone feel lonely and left on their own, by taking their friends away from them. And they may e-bully, by sending nasty emails or text messages.

Avoid e-bullying on ➡ mobile phones. Be careful who you give your phone number to.

THINK IT THROUGH

Is physical bullying more serious than non-physical bullying?

Yes. As they say, 'Sticks and stones can break my bones, but words can never hurt me'.

No. All forms of bullying hurt people. Words may not break bones, but they can really hurt someone's **self-esteem**.

What do YOU think?

Spotting the signs

How can people know if someone is being bullied – and what can they do to help?

People often do not like to admit that they are being bullied. They may feel afraid, or stupid and weak. Perhaps they think that no one can help them. A bully often relies on the fact that their **victim** will not 'tell' because, that way, the bully stays in control. But there are many signs to look out for which may show that someone is being bullied. If you can spot the signs, you can help to stop the bullying.

Physical signs

Scratches, cuts and bruises are one sign that someone may be being bullied – especially if there is no real explanation for how the person got them. Victims of bullying may also not have any dinner money at school, or pocket money, because it has been stolen or they have been forced to hand it over. Their belongings, such as their mobile phone or school bag, may also go missing, or their clothes may be ripped.

People who are bullied often feel ill, or say that they feel ill, so that they do not have to go to school or to other places where they may get bullied. Occasionally, they may run away from home to get away from the problem, or even try to kill themselves. Victims of bullying need – and deserve – lots of help.

◐ Scratches and bruises may be a sign that someone is being bullied.

Acting up

It is not always easy to tell if someone is being bullied by the way they act. Sometimes, victims of bullying become very quiet, and they draw away from other people. But they may act in the opposite way, too – by getting bad-tempered and moody. They may easily get fed up with people at school or home, and shout at or fight with them. Yet underneath all these different ways of behaving, people who are bullied share many feelings. They feel unhappy, worried, frightened – and alone.

TOP TIPS

If you think that someone is being bullied, you could help them by:

◎ being friendly to them and letting them know that you care

◎ spending time with them, say, at breaktimes at school

◎ listening to them and understanding how they feel

◎ telling a trusted person about the bullying, and asking for help.

THINK IT THROUGH

If you think that someone is being bullied, should you step in to help?

Yes. The person who is being bullied needs help from other people, so they know that they are not alone.

No. Getting involved might be risky. It's the victim's problem, not mine.

What do YOU think?

Why bully?

What makes people bully others?

All sorts of people bully others, for all sorts of reasons. But there is never any excuse for bullying, and people who get involved with bullying can – and should – change their behaviour.

Measuring up

Young people often look at people around them to see how they measure up. If they think that someone else is 'better' than them – cleverer or more sporty – they may feel jealous. They may start to bully them because it makes them feel stronger. If they decide that someone else is 'worse' than them, they may pick on their so-called 'faults' – anything from having ginger hair to being disabled. And yet the truth is that no one is any better or any worse than anyone else. We are all different, and we all have good and bad points. Most importantly, we all deserve to be treated with respect.

Some people bully ➲ because they are afraid of getting picked on – and so they pick on other people first.

Power trip

Most bullies feel more powerful when they pick on other people. A small number of people who bully may even have low **self-esteem**, which means that they feel bad about themselves. They may only feel good about themselves when they are bullying, because they think that this makes them look 'big' in front of their friends. But low self-esteem is not an excuse – bullying is always wrong.

TOP TIPS

People who bully others can – and do – change. Here are some things that a bully needs to think about:

◎ Why am I bullying? Is it fair to take out my problems on other people?

◎ Bullying hurts. Would I like to feel the sort of pain I'm giving to others?

◎ I can be helped to stop bullying – by talking to someone I really trust.

◎ If I stop bullying, I will feel much better – and happier.

⬆ People can stop their bullying behaviour. Most people who used to bully others grow up to become loving friends and parents.

THINK IT THROUGH

Is there any excuse for bullying?

Yes. Maybe the bully has learned to bully, because they have been bullied themselves. They may not know any better.

No. Bullying is always wrong. Even if the bully has problems, they should get help rather than take their problems out on other people.

What do YOU think?

Picking on differences

What's so wrong about people being different?

Are you tall or short? Do you like Maths or English? Is your favourite sport cricket or tennis? How about music – do you prefer pop or rock? People all over the world look and speak differently, and have many different tastes. People who bully others often dislike and pick on these differences. And yet, we should enjoy our differences – they make each of us special, and they make life much more fun!

Nitpicking

Bullies can get easily irritated by other people. They find all sorts of excuses to pick on them, from the way they look and the clothes they wear to their personality. They only ever notice the differences between people. If they looked for things in common, they would see a whole different picture.

Top thoughts

'All the people like us are We,
And everyone else is They.'

Rudyard Kipling, author (1865–1936)

I'm not playing with him! Stripey T-shirts are stupid!

I'm not playing with him! How can anyone wear stripey trousers?!

The big issues

People who bully others don't just pick on little things – they go for the big stuff, too. Some people bully others who are of a different **race**. **Racism** is **illegal** in many countries, including the UK and Australia.

Bullying because of disability is also a problem. Some bullies pick on people with disabilities – such as those in a wheelchair – because they think that they are weak. If they looked at the person behind the disability, rather than at the disability itself, they would discover someone who is fun and interesting to know.

↻ Racist bullying is wrong, and it is against the **law**. If you see racism happening, don't join in – tell a teacher, parent or carer about what you have seen.

THINK IT THROUGH

Is it OK to treat people differently if they are not the same as you?

Yes. It can be hard to understand people who are different to you, so how can you treat them the same?

No. Everyone is different, anyway! Even if people are similar in some ways, they will be different in others. We all have the right to be treated the same.

What do YOU think?

How does speaking out help to stop bullying?

Telling someone if you are being bullied – or if you think that someone else is being bullied – is one of the best ways to stop it from happening. It may be scary – but speaking out against bullying can change lives.

Keeping secrets

People who are bullied often feel afraid. They may worry that telling someone else about the bullying will only make it worse. Sometimes, they feel ashamed about speaking out. Perhaps they believe that they should be able to deal with the bullying alone – and so they stay quiet. Remember – everyone has the right to be safe from bullying, and speaking out is one of the best ways to stop it.

Victims of bullying find it helpful to talk to someone they trust about the problem, and to come up with solutions together.

Top thoughts

'A problem shared is a problem halved.'

Traditional saying

Talk time

Who could you speak to about bullying?

 Maribel: You could speak to a friend – someone you can trust.

 ali: Yeah, or to your parents, or a brother or sister.

Lauren: If it's happening at school, you could talk to a teacher or the headteacher.

 Tyrone: Or to the playground supervisor at breaktimes.

Sharing the problem

Sharing problems makes people feel less alone. People who are being bullied should speak to someone they really trust. It may be a family member, such as a grandparent, someone at school, or a friend. In the UK and Australia, there are several bullying helplines, which people can call or email for support and advice. In the Getting help box on page 31, you will find details of how you can get support at any time.

Writing things down can really help 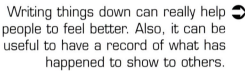 people to feel better. Also, it can be useful to have a record of what has happened to show to others.

TOP TIPS

If you are being bullied, talking to someone you really trust means that you can sort things out together. Follow these top tips for getting started:

◎ It can help to practise what you want to say in advance. Try writing it down first.

◎ Remember to tell the whole story – what has happened to you, where and when it happened, how often, who did it and who saw it happening.

◎ Be prepared to speak out clearly if the person you talk to suggests doing something that you think will make things worse.

Newsflash

The UK government is planning to make it easier for people to speak out against bullying. As part of their plans, a hard-hitting film called 'Tell Someone' will be shown on TV and in cinemas. The film gives details of an anti-bullying website set up by the government, as well as the number for ChildLine. The government hopes that the film will help children to find it easier to tell an adult or someone else if they are being bullied.

What can victims of bullying do to stay safe?

People who spend time with other people are less likely to be bullied.

People who are being bullied often feel that there is nothing they can do to stop the bullying. They may feel too afraid to deal with the problem. No one deserves to be bullied – but people who are being bullied do need and deserve to be given help. As well as getting support from others, there are some things that **victims** of bullying can do to help themselves, too.

Safety in numbers

You may have heard people talk about 'safety in numbers'. This means that people are less likely to be get picked on if they stick with other people. People who are alone a lot are more likely to be bullied. Being with even just one or two other people may make people think twice about bullying you.

If you find it hard to make friends, try out the top tips below.

TOP TIPS

Being with friends can help to prevent bullying. These are some of the things that young people say makes a good friend. Try some of them out, if you can! A good friend:

◎ is kind, and interested in other people
◎ laughs when someone tells a joke
◎ suggests doing things together
◎ helps other people out.

EARLY YEARS

Research for assignments should be from a variety of sources e.g. books, magazines and websites. At the Library, you can borrow up to **8 resources** for up to **3 week** and we have the following resources available:

YOU CAN ALSO ACCESS YOUR SUBJECT GUIDE ONLINE

Scan the QR above to access now

Extra Information:

Your Library Team = Kath Herrington & Elisa Neath

Open 8:30-17:00 (16:30 close Fridays)

Ask for help, contact **library@weston. ac.uk**

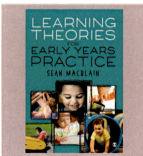

LibraryPlus

Don't go there

There may be places where bullies often hang out – for example, in the local park, on the way to school or on the school bus. Victims of bullying can protect themselves by avoiding these places. They may be able to find a different route to school, or choose not to go to the park until the bullying stops. If it is impossible to avoid certain places, being with other people will help. Walking to school with friends, or sitting near the driver on the school bus, can be a good idea.

Self-defence

People who are bullied should never fight back physically. Instead, they should walk away from the bullying whenever they can. Learning a form of **martial arts**, such as judo or karate, is a great way to feel safe. People who know how to defend themselves feel more confident, and they learn how to get out of tricky situations without getting into a fight. It is a great way to make new friends, too!

Stay close to an adult when you are on the school bus or in the playground at break times. This will make it difficult for a bully to continue to pick on you.

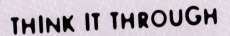

THINK IT THROUGH

Is it right that victims of bullying should keep away from certain places to avoid a bully?

Yes. It may be annoying, but it is worth it – to be safe. Once the bullying has stopped, you will be free to go wherever you like.

No. People should be free to go wherever they like. It's not fair to have to avoid places you would normally go to.

What do YOU think?

Being strong

How can people feel strong from the inside – and how can it protect them from bullying?

Being strong doesn't necessarily mean building strong muscles! People can be strong inside, even if they are physically small or weak. It is all to do with **self-esteem**. Bullying is never, ever the **victim**'s fault. But, if someone has low self-esteem, people might be more likely to pick on them. All victims of bullying need help and support from others – but thinking about self-esteem may help them to feel stronger themselves.

I'm OK

People with high self-esteem are happy with who they are, and this makes them feel strong inside. They accept themselves just as they are – with all their good points and all their not-so-good points! They realize that no one is perfect – and that that is OK. This kind of strength means that bullies can't upset or frighten them. They don't care if someone puts them down. And they feel more in control, because they can make their own decisions about who are good friends and who are not.

Everyone is special – and ➲ everyone deserves to be loved and respected, whoever they are.

You're OK

People who are strong inside realize that, even if they do not like someone, they can still treat them kindly. Victims of bullying sometimes find that the bullying stops if they treat the bully – as well as themselves – with respect, even though it might be difficult to do.

It's OK

Another way that victims of bullying can help themselves is to try to focus on the good things in their life – even small things, such as loving a pet or reading a favourite book. It can be easy to feel that the bullying is the only thing going on in their life. If they really think about it, they may see that it is not! And, even when something bad does happen, people can try to stay positive, rather than letting it get them down.

Top thoughts

'One kind word warms three winter months.'

Traditional Japanese saying

THINK IT THROUGH

Does thinking positively really change things?

Yes. It can be enough just to think positive thoughts, even if you don't feel them. Soon, your feelings will start to change, too – for the better!

No. If you try to pretend that everything is OK, it does not make it OK – or change the situation.

What do YOU think?

Think about all the good things in your life, such as your hobbies. It can help stop you worrying about the things that are not so good.

Face-to-face

What should people do when they are face-to-face with a bully?

Often, if you seem to ◑ stop caring about the bullying, the bullies lose interest. Then, things will get easier for you.

Have you ever been face-to-face with someone who is bullying you? It can be pretty scary. But there are lots of things that you may be able to do in this situation.

Get help

Some of the ideas given here may work for you – but don't worry if you cannot do them. Often, it can be too hard to handle a difficult situation alone. Anyone who is being bullied needs help from others, more than anything else. Talking to someone you trust is the very best thing you can do. Remember – you are not alone.

Keep cool

Facing a bully probably makes your heart race with nerves, but staying calm can help you to cope and to think more clearly. Sometimes, you can help to calm yourself down by taking a few really deep breaths. Don't worry if it does not work for you or if you forget – but it is always worth giving it a try, if you can.

Walk away

Sometimes, it is best to walk away from a bullying situation, without saying anything. Ignoring the person who is bullying gives them the message that they are not hurting or annoying you. This will make it more likely that the bullying will stop.

Be firm

At other times, it can be better to stand up to the bully – although it is important never to get into a fight. Fighting only make things worse, and people may get hurt. Being firm, and clearly telling the person to stop bullying, gives a strong message that the bully cannot control you.

Talk time

What kind of things could you say to someone who is bullying you?

ali: You could just say 'Stop bullying me' or 'Go away.'

Maribel: Or say, 'I don't like that.'

Lauren: You could ask them to think about what they are doing.

Tyrone: You need to sound confident, though. Look them in the eye and speak in a clear voice.

THINK IT THROUGH

Does it work to tell a bully to stop?

Yes. If you tell the person clearly to stop bullying you, it will show them that you won't put up with it.

No. Sometimes, the bully will not stop bullying you, even if you tell them to. It may be better to walk away.

What do YOU think?

Katie-Ann's story

Katie-Ann stood up to her bullies:

'I used to get called all sorts of names because I'm very small. Then my friends started to leave me because the bullies started having a go at them. I was lonely and I had low **self-esteem**. Since I stood up for myself, things have really improved. I have made new, loyal friends and I'm much more confident.'

Geek!

Well, at least I know I'll pass my test!

23

A helping hand

Can other people help someone who is being bullied?

Being bullied is horrible. Even if it is not happening to you, there is a lot you can do to help someone else who is being picked on. By working together, people can bring bullying to an end.

Talk time

How can you be a friend to someone who is being bullied?

Tyrone: First of all, you can refuse to join in with the bullying – and tell the bully to stop.

Lauren: You could ask the person how they are feeling, and be a good listener.

ali: Getting them to tell an adult about the bullying will help a lot. You could even go with them, or tell someone for them.

Maribel: Also, you could hang out with them at school, so they are safer.

◖ Just being there to listen, and to share problems and ideas, is a great way to be a friend to someone who is being bullied.

Being a friend

One of the most important ways you can help someone who is being bullied is to be friends with them. Most **victims** of bullying feel very lonely. Being friendly with them will help them in many ways. It will make them realize that there is nothing wrong with them, and that other people like them, even if the person who is bullying them doesn't. This will help to improve their **self-esteem**, which will make them feel more confident about dealing with being bullied.

Getting help

If you see someone being bullied, it will not help if you rush in to try to tackle the bullies. This could make things worse for everyone. If you can, get help from an adult quickly. You can also tell the person who is bullying to stop – and that you don't agree with what they are doing. Don't just walk away and leave it to others. And never be tempted to join in and bully, just because everyone else is.

You can help someone who is being bullied to talk to a trusted adult about their problem. Going along with them will make them feel more confident.

THINK IT THROUGH

Should people who are being bullied sort out the problem themselves?

Yes. They are the one with the problem, and it's up to them to make it go away.

No. Other people should help them. Bullying can be really scary – and so they need people on their side, too.

What do YOU think?

No to school bullying

Have you ever seen anyone being bullied at your school? Young people spend a lot of their time at school, and this makes it a place where bullying is more likely to happen. Schools are aware of this – and so they usually have different ways of tackling the problem. You, too, can get involved with stopping bullying at school.

Anti-bullying policies

Most schools in the UK and Australia have **anti-bullying policies**, which tell people what they should do if they, or someone they know, are being bullied at school. Young people and their parents can ask for a copy of their school's anti-bullying policy. Normally, it will tell them who they should speak to, for example, class teachers or the headteacher. It will also explain how the school will deal with the bullying problem, and how they will support **victims** of bullying.

Newsflash

Pupils at school who support those who are being bullied really help to stop it happening. Thousands of UK schoolchildren as young as six have already been specially taught how to help. They learn how to be a 'go-between', or **counsellor**, so they can sort out problems between those who are bullied and the bullies themselves. And they try to find out why there is a problem in the first place.

Most school anti-bullying policies encourage discussion between the pupil, parents and staff to sort out issues.

Getting involved

You can make a difference, too. Being part of your **school council** will mean that you can help to make decisions. You may be able to put forward your ideas about dealing with bullying. Some schools also teach pupils to be 'listeners', so that they can be there to support other pupils who are being bullied.

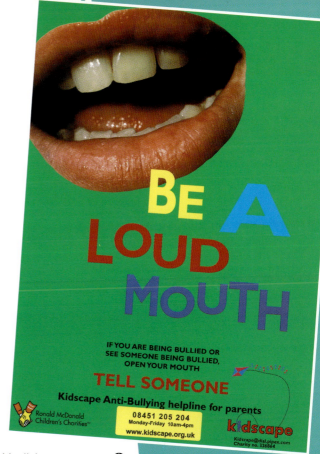

Anti-bullying posters 🎧 can help to prevent bullying at school.

TOP TIPS

Many schools have ways to help to stop bullying. Check out what your school says about it and, if necessary, suggest some of these ideas:

- ◎ a 'golden bench', where anyone who has a problem can sit down if they would like help
- ◎ 'bully boxes', where people can put a note if they are being bullied
- ◎ 'bully courts', where young people can work with teachers to come up with ideas to solve the bullying problem.

THINK IT THROUGH

Can young people really influence what happens at school?

Yes. Young people often have different thoughts and ideas to adults, and teachers often like to listen to them.

No. Teachers and headteachers make the rules – and children just have to follow them.

What do YOU think?

No more bullying

Fact Flash

Remember – if you are being bullied, and you feel that you can't cope, you can phone the numbers given in the Getting help box on page 31 for immediate help and support.

Because bullying is such a problem in many countries, such as the UK, the USA and Australia, many organizations have been set up to help people, and to advise on ways to tackle the problem. The **law** also supports people who are being bullied.

Safe support

Anti-bullying organizations are run by people who are specially trained to deal with bullying. In the UK, ChildLine, Bullying Online and Kidscape are examples of such organizations. In Australia, people can get in touch with anti-bullying organizations such as Bullying No Way. You can find details of these and other organizations on page 31.

Anti-bullying organizations are for anyone who is affected by bullying – including **victims** of bullying, families and friends who want to help, and even the bullies themselves. They provide information about bullying, including leaflets and real-life stories. Many of them also have helplines, which people can phone or email to get advice.

Helplines are phone ➲ numbers that people can call if they are having problems that they can't cope with alone. These lines can help everyone who is involved in bullying, from the victim to the bully themselves.

Bullying and the law

Bullying is wrong – and some things that bullies do are against the law. In the UK, there are laws to protect people from being pestered or hurt by other people, in person or by telephone. Forcing people to hand over their money or belongings is a form of stealing. Hitting or kicking is a form of **assault**. Anything that is against the law can be reported to the police, who will then deal with it.

Over to you!

Whether you are someone who is being bullied, someone who knows somebody else who is being bullied, or a bully yourself: you can bring bullying to an end. This book has lots of ideas about how to go about this. Remember – anyone can change! People who bully others can choose to be kinder. Victims of bullying can find places to get help. Everyone can choose to step in and not ignore bullying. Go on – help to make the world a better place!

Give bullying the boot!

Rebekah's story

Rebekah was being bullied at home by her step-sister. Here is her story:

'The bullying started when my mum got married again. My step-sister was older than me and I liked her a lot. But when she moved in, she started making fun of me, especially in front of her friends. She told me I was fat and ugly. Later, she started breaking my things and making me clean her room.

'I tried to talk to Mum, but I didn't want to make her unhappy. In the end, I phoned ChildLine and talked to a **counsellor**. She really took me seriously. She helped me to work out what to say to my mum and step-dad. My step-sister realized how much she had hurt me, and now we get on much better.'

Glossary

anti-bullying policy document that explains how schools will deal with bullying

assault violent physical or non-physical attack

counsellor someone who is properly trained to listen to and help people

depressed feeling negative about life, and feeling no hope that things will improve. People who feel very depressed should see a doctor to get help.

e-bullying when bullies use email, the Internet or mobile phones to bully others – for example, by sending nasty emails or text messages

humiliate to make someone feel 'small' or bad about themselves

illegal against the law

law set of rules that a whole community or country has to follow

martial arts sports (including judo and karate) that enable a person to physically defend or protect themselves

physical bullying when physical force, such as hitting or biting, is used to bully someone

non-physical bullying when bullies do not use physical force, but hurt people with words – such as insults – or use other methods, such as leaving people out or threatening them

race group of people from a particular place, who have particular physical characteristics or a particular way of living

racism treating someone badly because of their race or religion. Racism is illegal in many countries, including the UK and Australia.

school council group of students who help to make decisions about school issues

self-esteem the way people feel about themselves. If someone has high self-esteem, they feel good about and are proud of themselves.

threat/threaten when a bully scares their victim by saying they will do something nasty to them in the future

victim person who is hurt by something that another person does to them

Check it out

Check out these books and websites to find out more about bullying, and to get help and advice.

Books

Good and Bad: Bully, Janine Amos (Cherrytree Books, 2001)

Little Wise Guides: All About Bullying, Lesley Ely (Hodder, 2001)

What Do You Know About Bullying?, Pete Sanders (Franklin Watts, 2000)

Anti-bullying organizations

Anti-Bullying Network (UK): www.antibullying.net

Bullying Online (UK): www.bullying.co.uk

Bullying No Way! (Australia): www.bullyingnoway.com.au

ChildLine (UK): www.childline.org.uk
  tel. 0800 1111 (see Getting help below)

Kidscape (UK): www.kidscape.org.uk tel. 08451 205 204

Kids Help Line (Australia): www.kidshelp.com.au
  tel.1800 55 1800 (see Getting help box below)

Getting help

If you feel very worried or upset about a bullying problem, you may want to talk to someone urgently. You can speak to an adult you trust, or you can phone a helpline for support.

- In the UK, you can phone ChildLine on 0800 1111 (open 24 hours a day). Please remember that calls to 0800 numbers are free, and they do not show up on phone bills. You can also write to them at ChildLine, Freepost NATN1111, London E1 6BR

- In Australia, you can phone Kids Help Line on 1800 55 1800 (open 24 hours a day).

Remember – you do not have to be alone.

Index